Minster Lovell Hall
OXFORDSHIRE

A J TAYLOR CBE, MA, D Litt, Dir SA
Formerly Chief Inspector of Ancient Monuments

The ruins at Minster Lovell are those of a manor house built in the first half of the fifteenth century by William, seventh Baron of Tichmarsh. It was at least the second house to occupy the site, which had belonged to the Lovells since the twelfth century. The buildings of the manor house were arranged around a quadrangle, which on the south was open to the River Windrush. The principal remains are the great hall with its entrance porch and the southwest tower beside the river. The aerial view on page 10, the drawings on pages 8 and 17 and the plan on the centre pages will help you to follow the description of Minster Lovell Hall as it was built and as it can be seen today. This handbook also has a chapter on the history of the hall and the people who built it and lived in it.

The illustration above shows the coat of arms and crest of Francis Viscount Lovell, KG (about 1483), and is based, by kind permission of the Dean and Canons, on the contemporary Garter Stall Plate in St George's Chapel, Windsor.

ENGLISH HERITAGE · LONDON

CONTENTS

© *Crown Copyright 1958*
Formerly published by HMSO 1975
First published by English Heritage 1985, reprinted 1990, 1992, 1997, 1998, 2003, 2006
English Heritage, 1 Waterhouse Square, 138-142 Holborn London EC1N 2ST
Printed in England by the colourhouse
Dd. 004008225 12/06 C10 matrix 076368 04421
ISBN 1 85074 281 2

SUMMARY

The ruins at Minster Lovell are those of a manor house built in the first half of the fifteenth century by William, seventh Baron Lovell of Tichmarsh. It was at least the second house to occupy the site, which had belonged to the Lovells since the twelfth century. On the attainder of William's grandson, Francis Viscount Lovell, after the battle of Bosworth (1485), the property went to the Crown. It was subsequently bought (1602) by Sir Edward (afterwards Lord Justice) Coke, whose descendant Thomas Coke Earl of Leicester dismantled the buildings between 1740 and 1750. The remains were then left to fall into decay, though parts of them were being used for farm purposes until a much later date. In 1935 the ruins were placed in the care of the nation.

During the thirteenth and fourteenth centuries there was also at Minster Lovell a small alien priory dependent on the Benedictine abbey of Ivry in Normandy. There were never more than two monks in residence, the senior holding the title of prior and acting as the abbot of Ivry's agent or proctor in matters to do with the abbey's properties in England. In later times there has been confusion between the priory and the manor house. There was, however, no connection between them. The existence of the former was terminated on the seizure of the alien priories by the Crown some twenty or thirty years before the latter was built. The site of the priory house is not known; it may have lain to the west of the church, where there is reason to believe the land belonged to Ivry. Apart from this house, which was simply the dwelling of the prior and his fellow monk, there were no other monastic buildings at Minster Lovell.

The buildings of the manor house were arranged round a quadrangle, which on the south was open to the River Windrush. The principal remains are the great hall with its entrance porch and the southwest tower beside the river. Of the ranges forming the sides of the courtyard only foundations are left. Along the river side are foundations of a buttressed enclosing wall. The solar and private apartments were grouped to the west, the kitchen and service quarters to the east of the hall. The chapel, with what was probably a withdrawing room below, adjoined the hall on the north.

DESCRIPTION AND TOUR

The ruins seen across the River Windrush, with the southwest tower on the left

The aerial view on page 10, the drawings on pages 8 and 17 and the plan in the centre of this handbook will help you to follow the tour and understand the description of Minster Lovell Hall as it was built and as it can be seen. The glossary at the back of the book should be referred to for an explanation of technical terms.

Minster Lovell Hall is situated on the River Windrush, about half way between Witney and Burford. Akeman Street, the Roman road from Cirencester to Alchester, runs little more than a mile (1.6km) to the north, while the main Oxford–Gloucester road skirts the valley on the south. It lies less than 10 miles (16 km) from Woodstock, where the royal palace long ranked in importance with Windsor and Clarendon.

The church and manor house stand close together a little to the east of the village, where the high ground of

Wychwood Forest slopes down to the river. There was at one time an approach to the house from the southeast by a track along the valley from the direction of Witney. This crossed the Windrush about a quarter of a mile (400m) below the ruins at a point where remains of a stone bridge may be seen beside a modern footbridge. It is likely that this was originally the principal route to the house, as the only direct entrance to the courtyard was on this side; the formal entrance to the principal apartments from the north was probably the approach from the garden.

The buildings are arranged around three sides of a quadrangle, the fourth having been separated from the river by a buttressed wall. The principal apartments, dominated by the hall, are on the north. The west wing contained chambers; the east, divided into two

The porch and hall from the north, with the cobbled pathway in the foreground

roughly equal parts by a passage, contained the kitchen at its northern end, the remainder of the wing between the passage and the river being occupied by the stable.

To the east of the hall was a group of service buildings. On the north, facing an outer court, is a building of two storeys, the upper originally the chapel and the lower consisting of the formal entrance porch and an apartment lit by three square-headed and formerly traceried windows, entered from the west through a small lobby communicating with the dais (west) end of the hall. Two small buildings projected to the north and a vaulted gateway, now much mutilated, but probably contemporary with the house, led to the church and the chapel of St Cecilia.

Entrance porch

The porch, which is approached by a patterned cobbled pathway, has a two-compartment quadripartite vault (ceiling), the main ribs of which spring from attached shafts carried down to the level of stone seats which project from either wall. The floriated vault bosses are for the most part badly weathered, but one example with a rose and another with an oak-leaf design can be distinguished. Much of the plaster with which the walls and roof were finished remains on the east side, and traces of it can be seen on the infilling of the vault.

Hall

On the right, beyond the porch, is the hall, 50 by 26 ft (15 by 8 m). Its height of

40 ft (12 m) from the floor to the top of the wall seems disproportionately great. Opposite the doorway from the porch a similar but lower doorway, at the other end of the screens passage, communicated with the courtyard via an added passage. Both doors opened inwards, and are wider than the pair at the dais end of the hall which opened outwards. The wide opening in the centre of the east wall behind the screens led to the passage to the kitchen past the buttery, pantry and bakehouse (refer to the plan on page 13). From the smaller arch in the east wall (rebuilt in 1937) a short staircase led to a large upper room to the east, shown in the Buck engraving of 1729 to have been lit from the north by a transomed window of five lights (see the illustration on page 8).

The hall obtained its principal light from the pair of tall two-light cusped windows on the south, further light coming from two others set high in the north wall, clear of the roof of the chapel. The window glass is recorded to have contained a series of heraldic medallions of the Lovells and the families connected with them. The hall was warmed by an open fire in the centre. The Buck print shows no louvre, and it seems that advantage was taken of the abnormal height of the room to allow the smoke to be withdrawn by a cross-draught obtained through openings at the top of the end walls. The three openings in the east gable can still be seen.

South of the dais there is a door communicating with the main staircase to the solar (principal private apartment). From the foot of the stairs a slanting passage led to the larger of two rooms under the solar. The stairs were covered by a stone vault, above which there was a room reached by a flight of steps in the thickness of the wall, possibly the lord's treasury or muniment room.

Solar

The upper storey to the west of the hall was occupied by the solar. The print of 1729 shows this to have been lit from the north by a large two-light transomed window, containing tracery identical with that in the window of the northwest building. The entrance was in the southwest corner by the door communicating with the stairs from the hall. A door opposite (one of the jambs of which remains) opened into the northwest building, while a third door led up a short flight of steps to the chapel. The west wall contained the fireplace, part of which survives; it had a tall, hexagonal chimney, shown in the Buck print. The roof sprang from a moulded cornice which on the east wall remains intact.

Rooms under the solar

Beneath the solar were two rooms. The larger, to the south, was entered through the slanting passage at the foot of the stairs. The dressed stonework of the original fireplace on the east side was transferred, in the course of alterations which may possibly be those referred to in the King's Book of Payments in 1518, to a new fireplace in the opposite wall. The doorway to the northwest building, though in its original position, has been reconstructed, perhaps at the same time.

Of the smaller room only foundations remain. It was probably used in connection with the apartments on the north side of the hall, and may not have communicated with the larger room to the south. It would most naturally be approached from the door to the north end of the dais, and must have been lit from the west, as the print shows no window on the north side.

Northwest building and the hall, looking northwest across the site of the stable and kitchen

North front

On the north of the hall there were, in addition to the porch, two apartments on the ground floor. The doorway north of the dais leads directly into the smaller, a lobby measuring approximately 15½ by 9ft (4.7 by 2.7m). This gave access to all the northern rooms. To the west a doorway communicates with the smaller of the two rooms below the solar; another in the northwest corner seems to have led to a spiral staircase to the chapel and the upper part of a destroyed projecting wing.

The partition wall, with the doorway into the main room to the east, has perished, but one of the jambs and part of the lintel remain in position. There is a low, single-light window in the north-east corner; its skewed appearance is caused by the splay having been joined by the cross wall, which tapered to meet it.

The main room must originally have been of considerable beauty. Its three windows are shown by the Buck print to have contained two traceried lights, while the spandrels of the rear arches are ornamented with quatrefoils, a feature not repeated in other parts of the building.

In the centre of the south wall are the remains of a fireplace, the dressed stonework of which has been destroyed. After the house was dismantled the room was used for farm purposes, and the lower part of the window nearest the porch was cut away to form a door. The surviving paving is from the farm period.

The upper storey has been destroyed, except in so far as it was formed by the north wall of the hall. But it seems clear, both from the fenestration, as drawn by the Bucks, and from its orientation, that it was the chapel.

At the west end, over the lobby, there was a small ante room; two of the corbels which supported its floor may be seen from below. The entrance was in the

The north front in 1729; an engraving by Samuel and Nathaniel Buck

south side, and was approached from the solar up six shallow steps in the thickness of the wall; there may also have been a door from the destroyed staircase at the northwest corner.

The chapel proper can best be pictured with the help of the 1729 drawing, which shows a typical perpendicular east window of three lights and a range of four three-light windows towards the forecourt, all closely resembling those in the church. Its lead roof was low pitched and would not obscure the windows of the hall. It was of six bays, covering chapel and ante chapel without a break; four of the massive corbels on which rested the principal rafters remain.

At a later period the room ceased to be used as a chapel, and certain structural alterations were made. The open timber roof was replaced by a ceiling, carried by four cross-beams, the ends of which were embedded in the walls, and the spacing of the holes shows that, unlike the original roof, it was planned in symmetrical relation to the windows. At the same time a fireplace was added, the insertion of the flue involving the removal of one of the original corbels.

A spiral staircase in the northwest corner of the hall led up to the roofs of both hall and chapel. Access to it was by a wall passage along the west side of the ante chapel connecting with the destroyed lower stairs from the lobby.

Northwest building

When the remainder of the house was dismantled, the building between the solar and the west wing continued in use. Until towards the middle of the nineteenth century it served as a barn, a door large enough to admit carts being cut in each side. This led eventually to the collapse of the roof, with the whole of the south wall and most of the north. Afterwards a cottage was constructed within the eastern half of the building; its slight foundations have now been removed, leaving as the only evidence of its existence a small fireplace built into the north wall and the partial blocking of the adjoining window.

The building closely resembled the solar wing, having two rooms below and one above. The ground-floor rooms were low, their two-light windows having flat timber heads and simple splayed openings; the entrance was through the small door from the solar wing. There was probably a fireplace on the south side of the larger room; in the smaller the fireplace is in the northwest corner, the flue being contrived in the angle of the wall and the slope of the west gable, which was surmounted by twin octagonal chimneys, one of them serving the adjoining room to the south.

The west wall of the upper room contains a two-light transomed window, each compartment having a cinquefoiled ogee head with quatrefoils in the angles of the cusping. The rear arch has a concave chamfer which is continued down to sill level; the spandrels are unornamented. One side of a double stone window seat remains intact, and beneath it is a square hole which carried the main upper-floor beam above the smaller ground-floor room. Besides the west window, there are the mouldings and splay of another on the north side.

The room was entered from the solar; one of the door jambs may be seen immediately above the reconstructed lower entrance, Adjoining the southeast corner of the ground-floor room are the foundations of a small added building which probaby contained garderobes (latrines).

SKYSCAN

Aerial view of Minster Lovell Hall with the southwest tower on the left, the hall on the right and the stable and kitchen in the foreground

West wing

The west wing contained five ground-floor rooms. Fireplaces, or traces of them, remain in the outer wall of the three northern rooms, the centre one of which also retains the threshold of a door from the courtyard. At the south end of the range there was a garderobe pit, with outlet to the river. Of the upper floor nothing but the south gable is left. This contains a two-light cusped window, from which the mullion has been lost.

At a later period a stone-lined tank was constructed in the room at the north end of the wing. It appears to have been used in connection with the well sunk in the courtyard near by. A new doorway was made giving access to the well and courtyard. The water was drawn off from the tank through a stone pipe and conveyed by a short covered channel to the outside of the wing. Here there was added a small rectangular building, of which only the foundations have survived.

These developments are possibly to be connected with the establishment of a small tanning industry. A lease of the manor in 1536 to Alexander Umpton of Wadley, Berkshire, mentions a building called the outer tanhouse, *le Tannehouse exteriori*. If, as seems possible, this refers to the small block built on to the outside of the west wing, the works must have been carried out before the date of the lease.

Southwest tower

At the southeast angle of the west wing is a tower which is not a part of the original plan. This addition involved the rebuilding of the southeast corner of the wing. A door was made in the end wall at first-floor level to give access to the staircase which led to the two upper floors of the tower. At the side of this doorway, and at a slightly lower level, a straight joint in the masonry marks the position of the jamb of a second door. This served the first floor of the tower and was reached by external stairs from the courtyard; from the top of these a short rise led to the foot of the existing stairs to the other floors. Here there was a landing carried on timber joists, the two holes for which remain some 4 ft (1.2 m) above the west-wing floor level. In order to strengthen the tower and support overhanging stone-work it has been found necessary to fill in the site of the door to the first floor.

The tower is of four storeys. Most of the north and south and the whole of the east wall have been destroyed, but on the west only the battlements are missing. On the ground floor there were garde-robes; the pit is on the side nearest the river. Adjoining it were two compart-ments, divided by a wall of which the upper part was carried across the pit to give additional support to the floor above. There is a single trefoiled light on the west; the opening on the north is modern.

As already indicated, access to the first floor was by external stairs. A slight offset marks the floor level; there are a single window on the west and part of a window splay on the south. The two upper floors were reached by the octagonal stair turret in the angle between the tower and the west wing and are marked off from those below by a moulded string course. The second-floor room was not more than 8½ ft (2.6m) in height and had peculiar fenestration. To the right of a low two-or three-light window, the splay of which can be seen in the south wall, there is a small quatre-foil set in a wide embrasure.

The third floor contained a finely pro-portioned chamber. The principal feature was an oriel window facing south, of which one splay and a small trefoiled tracery light remain. The embrasure was carried down to the floor, the level of which is indicated by a series of beam

holes. There are also traces of a window on the north. The walls were finished with battlements, below which there is a moulded string course decorated with grotesque heads. On the turret, which rises from a finely carved corbel, the battlements still survive,

Between the tower and the end of the east wing the quadrangle was protected against flooding by a buttressed retaining wall, the base of which may be seen con-tinuing the line of the south side of the tower. Further east it has been destroyed altogether. A massive foundation protects the end of the east wing; from its align-ment it appears to be related to the earlier buildings, the outline of which is marked on the ground a little to the north.

East wing

Excavation has made it possible to trace the greater part of the plan of the east wing. At the north end, where founda-tions are missing, the story can to some extent be completed with the help of the Buck illustration. The south end was occupied by the stable, in which, as the pitched floor shows, there were two rows of stalls ranged on either side of a central alleyway, along one side of which ran a narrow gutter.

The lease to Alexander Umpton in 1536 mentions a stable by the great gate *(stabulum iuxta magnam portam)*. If this may be identified with the stable in the east wing, it leaves little room for doubt that the 7 ft (2.1 m) wide passage to the north of the stable formed the principal entry to the house. It is floored with rough rubble pitching which from the inner end is continued towards the south-west door of the hall.

The kitchen was distinguished from the rest of the wing by its thick south

Churchyard wall

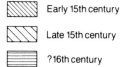

	Early 15th century
	Late 15th century
	?16th century
	18th century and later
	Uncertain

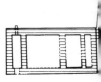

0   5   10   20   30
Metres

0 10 20 30 40 50   100
Feet

River Wi

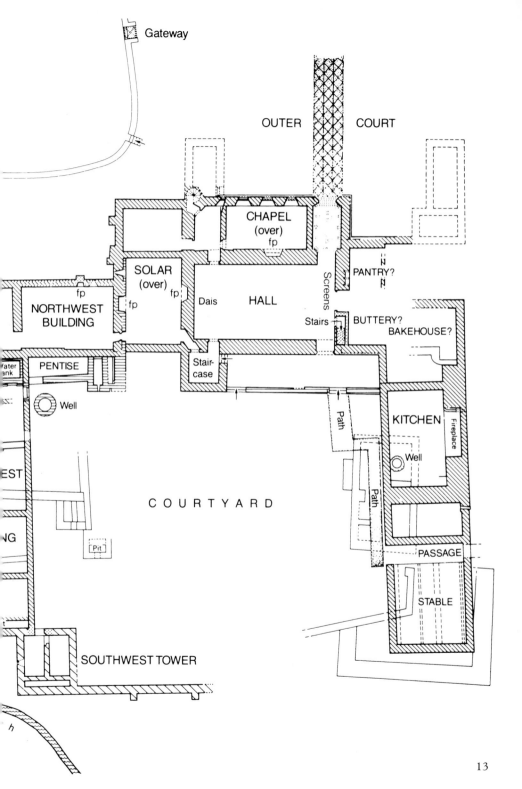

Gateway

OUTER COURT

CHAPEL (over) fp

SOLAR (over) fp

fp

NORTHWEST BUILDING

fp

Dais

HALL

Screens

PANTRY?

N

Stairs

BUTTERY?

BAKEHOUSE?

ater ank

PENTISE

Stair-case

Well

KITCHEN

Fireplace

EST

Well

NG

C O U R T Y A R D

Path

Path

Pit

PASSAGE

STABLE

SOUTHWEST TOWER

and east walls. The latter still has the hearth of the range fire, and there was a second range on the south. Close to the west wall is the well.

The 1729 drawing shows that north of the kitchen there were two buildings of roughly equal width, with twin gables running north and south. The outer building is shown with a chimney at the south end. The arrangement of the inner one, which adjoined the hall, can in part be reconstructed.

On either side of the door from the hall a small area was probably partitioned off to form the pantry on the north and the buttery on the south. In the former the remains of a cupboard, with a shelf and centre division, can be seen. A short length of foundation 15in (38cm) in thickness suggests the partitions were of timber construction. Between them was the passage to the kitchen. Above was a room reached by the stairs from the screens passage. Its high-pitched roof was of two bays; the corbel supporting the centre principal and the indents of the rafters remain on the wall of the hall. A square-headed transomed window of five lights filled the north side.

Periods of building

Clearance of the site 1937-39 brought to light traces of a number of earlier buildings, but the associated finds were not sufficient to provide any satisfactory evidence of their date. They comprise two groups of foundations the common alignment of which suggests that they were contemporary. One partly occupied the site of the later kitchen; the other, part of the ground afterwards covered by the west wing.

On the south side of the former there was a paved entrance, approximately on the line of the later passage through the

east wing; south of this again ran what appears to have been the enclosing wall of a courtyard.

The work is unlikely to be earlier than the second half of the thirteenth century, and may perhaps be tentatively ascribed either to the John Lovell (died 1287) who in 1273 founded the chantry of St Cecilia, or to his son, also John, who in 1291 was permitted to enclose a part of the forest of Wychwood pertaining to the manor.

The three sides of the quadrangle and the gate to the church belong stylistically to the first half of the fifteenth century and, for reasons already set forth, may perhaps be dated more closely to the period 1430-40. The southwest tower, with the adjacent river wall, is an addition probably of the last quarter of the same century. It is tempting to see in it the hand of Richard of Gloucester's favourite, Francis Viscount Lovell, who was supposed to have returned to Minster after the battle of Stoke (1487). The period between 1477 and 1485, when he escaped to Flanders from the field of Bosworth, is the most likely time for such work to have been undertaken. Reasons have been given for assigning the outer buildings by the west wing, the water tank, and the second wall to a date before 1536; the added passage on the south side of the hall, with the alterations in the room under the solar and the addition of a pentise against the north-west building, may belong to the same period.

Finally there are the alterations involved in the conversion of the chapel to domestic uses. Nothing is left in the building itself to show when this took place, but it would be natural to regard it as a post-Reformation development and to attribute it to the second half of the sixteenth century.

Occupation of the northwest building

The dovecote

Interior of the roof of the dovecote

continued, with effects on its fabric already described, until well into the nineteenth century. The period following the dismantling of the house also saw the erection in the middle of the courtyard of buildings of uncertain purpose, the foundations of which were disclosed by excavation.

Dovecote

The manorial farm with its attendant yards and buildings lay to the northeast of the hall. Some of the buildings still there are of medieval date and probably survive from the fifteenth century. Among them is the manorial dovecote, a small circular building with a conical roof.

The pigeons entered through a central hole in the roof, originally covered by a louvre. The internal walls are lined with tiers of nesting boxes in which the young birds, or squabs, were reared before ending their days in the kitchen.

The dovecote came into the care of the nation in 1957, since when it has been carefully repaired and renovated. It can be reached by way of the path which skirts the private land and buildings on the river side.

HISTORY

The village of Minster takes its name from the church. The 'minster' [Latin *monasterium*, used in the sense of a church served by a small body of secular priests rather than of a community bound by monastic rule] was dedicated to the young martyr prince Kenelm, son of Kenwulf, King of Mercia. Kenelm is traditionally held to have been murdered in AD819 near Halesowen and buried at Winchcombe, and the foundation of the church cannot therefore be earlier than the first half of the ninth century. The areas served by the old minsters were large, and St Kenelm's probably became the centre of an ecclesiastical district embracing many manors, for smaller groups of which separate parishes were gradually formed in later times.

The name Lovell was not attached to Minster till late in the thirteenth century, when it begins to be used to distinguish the manor of which the Lovells were lords from the adjacent manor of Little Minster, then held by the Earls of Pembroke. When it came into the Lovells' possession is uncertain, but William Lupellus, the first Lovell, received considerable grants of land in England from Henry I in or after 1124. He was assessed to Danegeld in Oxfordshire in 1130, and it is likely that one of these grants included Minster. William was the grandson of Robert, Lord of Ivry. Through his son and successor Waleran d'Ivry, a benefactor of Ivry Abbey, his English lands passed in or about 1177 to his nephew, William Lovell, who is mentioned in 1193 as one of the English knights of the Third Crusade. The manor of Minster, held in dower, was granted him by his mother

Maud, who, at some date not later than 1184, gave to Ivry Abbey the Church of Minster Lovell, which thereby became a small alien priory.

After the final seizure of the alien priories by the Crown in 1414, the Ivry property was granted to Henry VI's new foundation at Eton, but the tradition of the priory long survived. When, however, early in the eighteenth century, the Buck brothers came to make their drawing of the manor the site of the priory house had been forgotten and the print was wrongly entitled 'Minster Lovell Priory.' The engraving reproduced on page 8, which is a valuable source of information about the former appearance of the buildings from the north, has thus helped to perpetuate a common misconception about their original function and purpose.

The wealth and prosperity of the Lovells in the later Middle Ages can be traced to the time of the John Lovell who succeeded to the family estates in Norfolk, Suffolk, Oxfordshire and Wiltshire in 1252, and who married Maud de Sydenham, heiress of Sir William de Sydenham of Tichmarsh, Northamptonshire. After this marriage Tichmarsh became the Lovells' principal seat, but the continuance of their interest in Minster is reflected in the endowment by John Lovell in 1273 of a chantry priest to say mass for the souls of himself and his wife and mother and father, 'either in the chapel of St Cecilia in the cemetery of Minster church or at the altar of the Blessed Virgin Mary within the church itself.' [The present farmhouse, which noticeably projects into the northwest corner of the churchyard, probably occupies the site of the chapel of St

Minster Lovell Hall as it might have been in the fifteenth century; a reconstruction illustration by Alan Sorrell

Cecilia; its south and west walls incorporate early masonry and may belong to the original building.]

John's successor was another John, who served with Edward I in Wales in 1277. In 1294 he was on the King's service in Gascony and in 1296 was marshal of the army in Scotland. From 1299 until 1307 he was summoned to Parliament by writs directed to John Lovell of Tichmarsh, whereby he is held to have become the first Lord Lovell. He served in Scotland in 1303 and 1304 and to him were surrendered the keys of Stirling Castle after its three months' siege. His son John Lovell, who succeeded him in 1310, was killed four years later at the battle of Bannockburn. This second Lord Lovell married Maud, the sister and heir of Edward Lord Burnell, and although in law the Burnell title passed to the descendants of her second husband, Sir John Haudlo, the Lovells persisted in their claim to the barony.

It is likely that during the middle of the fourteenth century Minster Lovell was being used as the regular residence of the family, for an inquiry of 1361 shows that the castle and buildings at Tichmarsh were then 'ruinous and destroyed,' and in 1364 the fifth baron is referred to as 'John Lovell of Co. Oxford.' He married Maud, the daughter and heiress of Robert de Holand, who on the death of her grandfather Robert Lord Holand became Baroness Holand, and in 1380 he is styled John Lovell, Knight, Lord of Tichmarsh and Holand. In 1391 he was taking proceedings against evil doers who had 'prevented him from reaching his house at Minsterlovell.'

In 1408 the inheritance passed to the eldest son, John, who became the sixth Lord Lovell, but Minster was assigned in dower and so continued in the possession of his mother the Lady Maud. John held the title for six years only, being suc-ceeded in 1414 by his son William. William did not enter into the full inheritance until the death of his grandmother in 1423, on which he succeeded to the barony of Holand. Baron Lovell and Holand and claimant to the barony of Burnell, had married in 1422 Alice, daughter of Sir John Deincourt, heiress to the baronies of Deincourt and Grey of Rotherfield. He was thus a great landholder and an extremely rich man, facts which are reflected in the scale of his buildings at Minster Lovell.

The old manor house was still standing in 1423, when it is recorded as consisting of a hall and four *camere*, with two barns, a stable, and farm buildings. How soon after this Lord William began to build is uncertain. He was serving in the French wars at intervals until 1431, and it may have been on his return in that year that he planned the new mansion.

In 1440 he obtained royal licence 'to impark a parcel of land called Minstrewodes, with two fields adjacent to the woods belonging to his manor of Minstrelovell, notwithstanding that the woods and fields are within the perambulation of the king's forest of Whichewode.' The making of the park may be an indication that the buildings were by this time nearing completion. It is significant, too, that shortly before the date of this licence Lovell had parted with his Norfolk manors of Billingford, Southmere, and Docking. Two years later, in 1442, he received licence 'to disafforest his woods called Minstrewodes with two fields thereto adjoining ... and to hold the same as a free chase and keep it by his own keepers to the exclusion of the king's forest officers,' with permission to enclose the woods and fields at will. Such evidence as there is, therefore, would suggest the years between 1431 and 1442 as the most likely period for the building of the mansion.

William Lovell died in 1455. His son and successor John, the eighth baron, was a prominent Lancastrian, and was made master forester of Wychwood for his services to Henry VI. Francis, the ninth baron, whom contemporary rhyme and later legend have combined to make the best known of all the Lovells, was the last of his line. A minor at the time of his father's death, when he came of age he threw in his lot with the Yorkists, and rose to high favour with Richard of Gloucester, who as Richard III created him Viscount Lovell in 1483. He held the offices of Constable of Wallingford Castle, Chamberlain of the Household, and Chief Butler of England, and was in a position of the greatest power.

After fighting on Richard's side at Bosworth Field in 1485, he escaped to Flanders, returning two years later to take part in Lambert Simnel's rebellion. He is generally held to have been killed at the battle of Stoke, near Newark, in June 1487; but according to Francis Bacon, 'there went a report that he fled, and swam over Trent on horseback but could not recover the other side ... and so was drowned.... But another report leaves him not there, but that he lived long after in a cave or vault.'

Some confirmation of the second version of his end comes from a letter written in 1737 by William Cowper, clerk of the Parliament, to Francis Peck, in his day a reputable antiquary:

Apropos to this, on the 6th May 1728, the present Duke of Rutland related in my hearing that, about twenty years then before (namely, in 1708, upon occasion of new laying a chimney at Minster Lovell), there was dis-covered a large vault or room underground, in which was the entire skeleton of a man, as having been sitting at a table, which was before him, with a book, paper, pen, etc., etc.;

in another part of the room lay a cap; all much mouldred and decayed. Which the family and others judged to be this Lord Lovell, whose exit hath hitherto been so uncertain.

The cellar, if cellar it was, has not been found again, but the story may none the less contain an element of truth and is worth the telling.

Lovell was attainted of high treason after Bosworth and his lands escheated to the Crown. They were granted in 1486 to Jasper Tudor, Duke of Bedford, who held them until his death in 1495, after which they again reverted to the Crown. Henry VII was at Minster Lovell in January 1494 and again in 1497 and 1503.

The various leases under which the manor was farmed during the sixteenth century tell us little of its history. We know from the King's Book of Payments that considerable sums were expended between February and November 1518 on 'the Reparations of Minster Lovell.' Unfortunately no hint is given as to what was done; the works are grouped with others at Ewelme, Woodstock, Cornbury, and Langley, and there is no distinction between the amounts laid out at each.

In 1602 the manor was purchased by Sir Edward Coke, at that time Attorney General. In the early years of the reign of James I, Coke was acquiring manors in many parts of the country and there is no reason to believe that he ever resided at Minster Lovell. At one time, however, there was a possibility that Minster might have become the Cokes' principal seat. In 1718 Thomas Coke, afterwards Earl of Leicester, spent part of his honeymoon here; he was in residence again in 1721, and in 1728 took for his first title the style of Lord Lovell of Minster Lovell. But any intention he may have had of residing permanently must have been given up before 1734, when William

Kent began to lay out the Cokes' new mansion at Holkham in Norfolk.

When Holkham was nearing completion Minster Lovell was abandoned, and in about 1747 the buildings were dismantled. The east and west ranges of the quadrangle and the kitchens to the east of the hall were demolished and no doubt became a quarry for building stone. The building to the west of the hall was converted into a barn; as Skelton's print shows, it was still roofed in the 1820s. An engraving of the year 1775 shows the ruins in very much the same condition as they appear today, and indeed little can have fallen or been destroyed since the initial demolition.

The Cokes remained lords of the manor until 1812, when it was sold to Sir W Elias Taunton, Recorder of Oxford and afterwards a Justice of the King's Bench. After his death in 1835 it passed through various hands and the estate was divided. That part of the property which included the remains of the manor house was purchased by Colonel la Terrière, whose widow, Mrs Agneta la Terrière, placed the ruins in the guardianship of the Commissioners of HM Works in 1935. Works of repair and conservation were undertaken by the Ancient Monuments Branch between that date and the outbreak of war in 1939.

GLOSSARY

Attainder   Forfeiture of an estate

Battlements   Indented parapet covering defenders from enemy observation and fire; crenellation; embrasure

Boss   Ornamental projection concealing the intersection of the ribs or beams of a vault or ceiling; ground prominence in hammered or carved work

Buttery   Room where liquor (especially ale) was stored

Buttress   Vertical projection from a wall to give additional strength or to resist the lateral thrust of an arch or roof

Chamfer   Surface formed by cutting off a squared edge, usually at an angle of 45 degrees

Cinquefoil   Five-lobed tracery

Corbel   Timber or stone projection from a wall to support a beam, etc

Cornice   Horizontal moulded projection crowning a building, especially the uppermost part of an *entablature*; ornamental moulding at the top of a column or round a room where walls and ceiling meet or at the top of a fireplace

Cusp   Point formed by the meeting of two foils or arcs in Gothic tracery (decorative stonework in a window)

Dais   Low platform for principal table in the great hall

Dressed plinth   See Plinth

Escheat   Confiscate; lapsing of property to the Crown or lord of the manor on the owner's dying intestate without heirs

Embrasure   Splayed opening in a wall for admitting light or shooting through; also used as the equivalent of crenellation (opening in the upper part of a parapet; battlement)

Entablature   Horizontal member above a classic column, often used without the column. It consists of three parts: the upper projecting cornice; the frieze, which when it swells outwards is said to be pulvinated; and the lower member, the architrave, which may be used as a frame for window, door or fireplace openings

Fenestration   Arrangement of windows

Garderobe   Latrine, normally discharging into a cesspit or through an outer wall into the moat or onto the berm (the space between the base of the wall and the moat)

Impark   Enclose land for a park; enclose in a park

Jamb   Side of an opening, doorway, window or fireplace

Light   Division of a traceried window, glazed or unglazed

Lintel   Stone or wooden headpiece of doorway or window opening

Mullion   Upright dividing a window or other opening into two or more lights; *transom* is the horizontal member

Muniment room   Room where documents (title deeds, etc) were preserved as evidence of rights or privileges

Ogee   Arch of continuous double curve, convex and pointed above and concave and bulbous below

Oriel   Small room or recess with a polygonal window, built out from a wall

Pentise   Penthouse; lean-to building or covered passage on gallery

Plinth   Projecting base of a wall or column, often chamfered or with decorative mouldings; *dressed plinth,* stone plinth with prepared shape and surface

Quatrefoil   Four-lobed tracery

Rear arch   Internal arch over door or window opening

Screens   Wooden partitions at the lower or kitchen end of a hall; between the screens and the kitchen, buttery and pantry lay the screens passage

Screens passage   Passage separating the great hall from the kitchen, buttery and pantry; the screens are wooden partitions

Shaft   Part of a column between base and capital; often one of a group of two or more clustered columns of lesser diameter; small or subordinate pillar

Solar   Private chamber, often bed-sitting room, at the upper end of the great hall and at a higher level than the hall floor; great chamber

Spandrel   Triangular area above the haunch of an arch; space between the shoulder of an arch and the surrounding mouldings

Spine-wall   Cross-wall on or close to the centre-line of a building

Splay   Diagonally cut-away surround of a window or doorway, in which the opening widens towards the face of the wall, thereby admitting more light and increasing the angle of view for observation or shooting through

Springing   Level at which an arch or vault rises from its supports

String course   Moulding or projecting band running horizontally across the façade of a building or around its walls

Tracery   Decorative branching stonework in the upper part of a window

Transom   Horizontal bar of wood or stone dividing a window or across the top of a doorway

Trefoil   Three-lobed tracery

Vault   Arched roof or ceiling in stone, sometimes relieved by stone ribs